TRUE OR FALSE?

RABBITS EAT THEIR OWN POOP

And Other Facts About Animals

JAN PAYNE AND STEVEN WILDER

Enslow Publishing
101 W. 23rd Street
Suite 240
New York, NY 10011
USA
enslow.com

Published in 2017 by Enslow Publishing, LLC.
101 W. 23rd Street, Suite 240, New York, NY 10011

Published in 2017 by Enslow Publishing, LLC, by permission of the Reader's Digest Association Inc., 44 South Broadway, White Plains, New York, 10601

Library of Congress Cataloging-in-Publication Data
Names: Payne, Jan. | Wilder, Steven.
Title: Rabbits eat their own poop : and other facts about animals / Jan Payne and Steven Wilder.
Description: New York, NY : Enslow Publishing, 2017. | Series: True or false? | Audience: Age 8-up. | Audience: Grade 4 to 6. | Includes bibliographical references and index.
Identifiers: LCCN 2016005250| ISBN 9780766077300 (library bound) | ISBN 9780766077287 (pbk.) | ISBN 9780766077294 (6-pack)
Subjects: LCSH: Animal behavior--Juvenile literature. | Animals--Juvenile literature.
Classification: LCC QL751.5 .P39 2017 | DDC 591.5--dc23
LC record available at http://lccn.loc.gov/2016005250

Printed in the United States of America

To Our Readers: We have done our best to make sure all website addresses in this book were active and appropriate when we went to press. However, the author and the publisher have no control over and assume no liability for the material available on those websites or on any websites they may link to. Any comments or suggestions can be sent by e-mail to customerservice@enslow.com.

Cover art by Joel R. Gennari

Interior illustrations by Paul Moran

Photo credits: maodoltee/Shutterstock.com (backgrounds throughout book); Nobelus/Shutterstock.com (dingbat on spine).

CONTENTS

Introduction

Did you know that a walrus can walk on its teeth? That bush babies drink their own pee? Or that a camel spits when it feels threatened? Or do they? This book is full of fascinating facts and formidable fictions. It's up to you to determine which is which.

From facts about deep sea creatures, to insects, to the pets we live with, you will have a great time testing your knowledge, learning some astonishing truths, and uncovering some large lies along the way. Then check out the shocking facts that follow to see if your lie-detecting skills are up to snuff.

IT'S UP TO YOU

Here's how it works. Each section contains a list of facts. On a separate sheet of paper, write down your answers. Then turn to page 44 and copy the chart. Write down your score for each section. Find out your grand total by adding up how many of these facts you got right!

So what are you waiting for? Grab a pencil and see if you can spot the twisted truths. Why not test your family and friends to see if they know the facts? You never know! You may surprise them with some of the stranger-than-fiction truths waiting to amaze you on these fun-packed pages.

Chapter One

BIZARRE BEASTIES

QUIZ

Why do animals do the things they do? Test your amazing animal expertise to see if you can tell the truths from the lies. On a separate sheet of paper, mark either True or False, then turn to pages 7–8 for the truth.

THE "FACTS"	TRUE	FALSE
1. Pill bugs drink through their bottoms.	☐	☐
2. Koalas never drink.	☐	☐
3. A fish called a pancake batfish can fly.	☐	☐
4. Dolphins can put one half of their brains to sleep.	☐	☐
5. Butterflies taste with their feet.	☐	☐
6. An ant never sleeps.	☐	☐
7. Ermines like to sing to their prey.	☐	☐

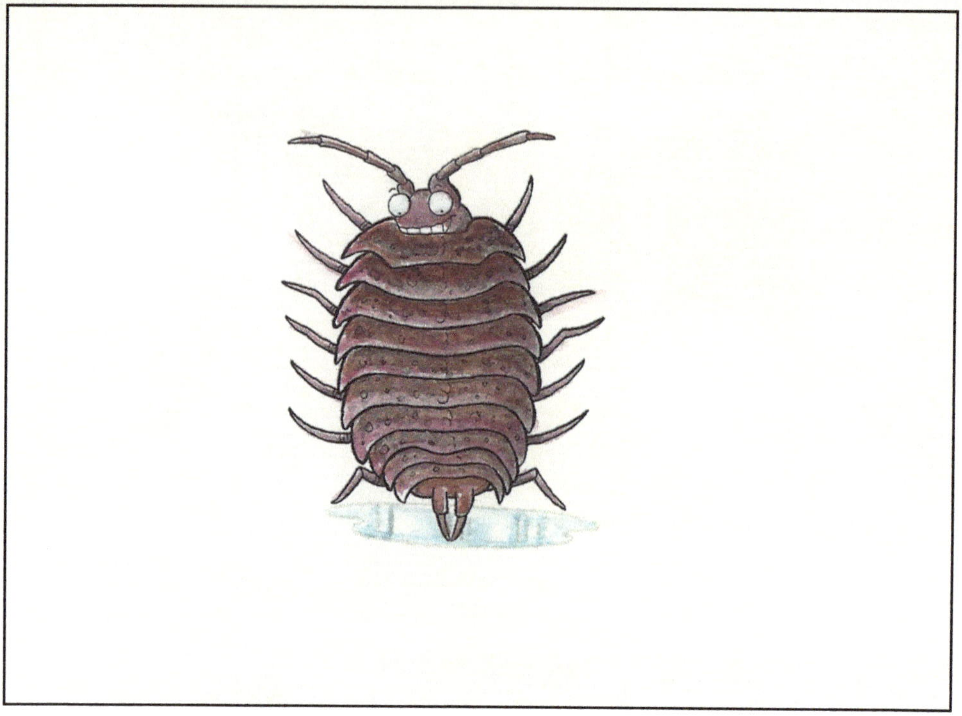

1. PILL BUGS DRINK THROUGH THEIR BOTTOMS.

TRUE

Pill bugs take in some water with their food, but when they are really thirsty, they drink through their bottoms. To vacuum up the water, they use things called uropods, which are little tubes positioned under their tails. The uropods suck up water when pressed together and held against moist surfaces.

2. KOALAS NEVER DRINK.

FALSE

Koala is an ancient native-Australian word meaning "no drink." In fact, koalas do occasionally take a sip of water, but they get most of their water from the leaves they eat. The leaves of the eucalyptus tree are their leafy snack of choice.

3. A FISH CALLED A PANCAKE BATFISH CAN FLY.

FALSE

The pancake batfish, a fish that lives in the deep waters of the Gulf of Mexico, can't fly. It can, however, "walk" on its fins. It has stubby fins, which the fish moves like legs, enabling it to hop around. Some people say the batfish looks like a pancake with feet.

4. DOLPHINS CAN PUT ONE HALF OF THEIR BRAINS TO SLEEP.

TRUE

Dolphins have to remain alert for days at a time to protect themselves from predators. To do this, they use a clever trick to stop themselves from getting tired. They put one half of their brains to sleep for a number of hours. When that half is rested, they wake it up and switch off the other half.

5. BUTTERFLIES TASTE WITH THEIR FEET.

TRUE

Butterflies have taste sensors on their feet, so they can tell if something is good to eat simply by standing on it. In fact, they don't even have mouths; once they find some nectar, they use a long tube named a proboscis to suck it out of flowers. Slurp!

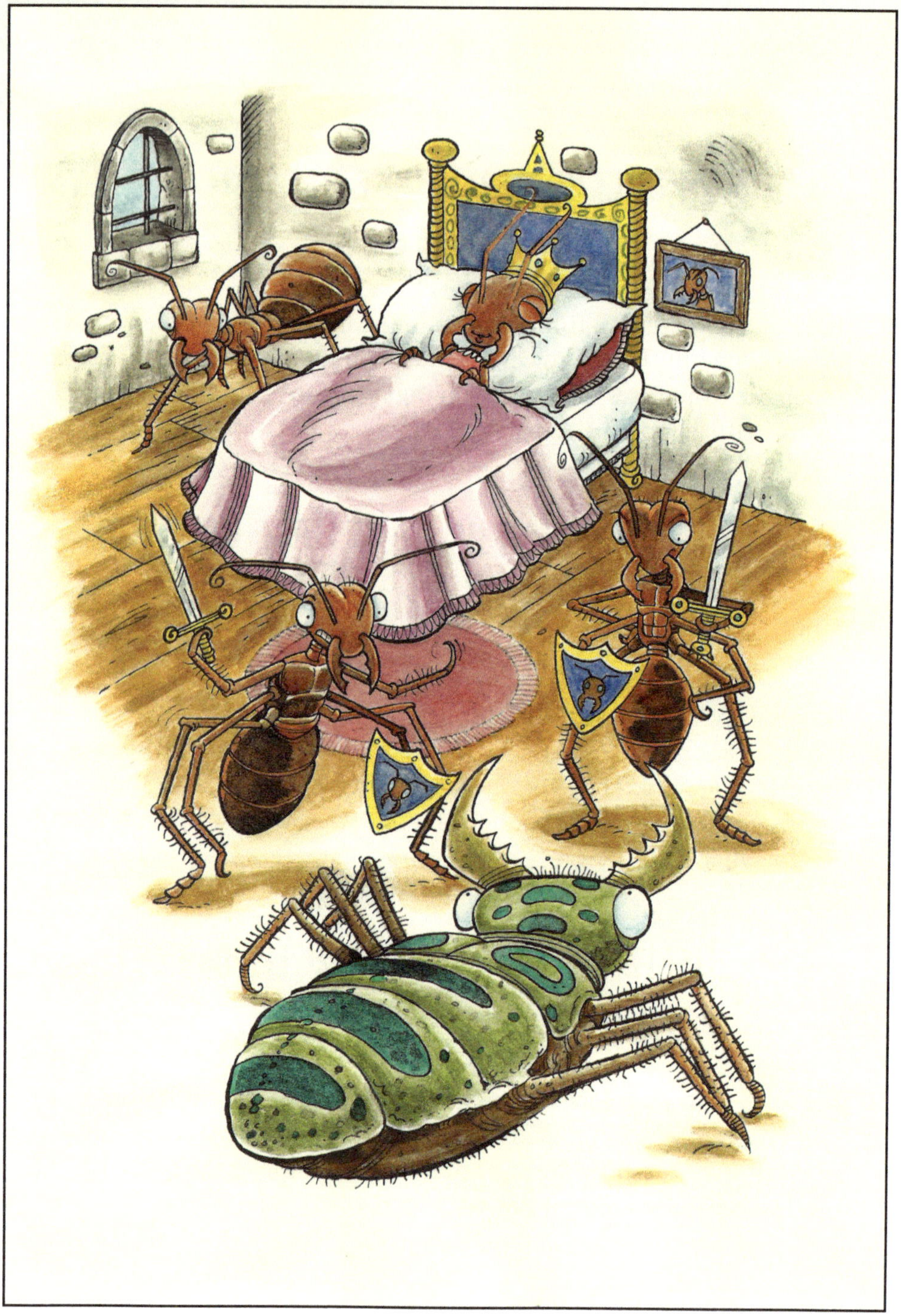

6. AN ANT NEVER SLEEPS.

FALSE

Actually, ants do sleep, but the ants in a colony are never all asleep at the same time. They take turns so there are always some awake to protect the nest. Ants take hundreds of short naps—as many as 250 a day—for about one minute at a time. The queen ant, on the other hand, gets luxury royal treatment and sleeps for up to nine hours a day.

7. ERMINES LIKE TO SING TO THEIR PREY.

FALSE

Ermines, which are related to weasels, are better dancers than they are singers. They hunt all kinds of animals, but they like nothing better than a tasty rabbit. When an ermine spots a rabbit, it does a kind of bizarre break-dance routine, with lots of leaps and twists, in order to get close to it. The rabbit becomes hypnotized by the ermine's crazy moves and stays rooted to the spot while the hunter boogies closer and closer, until it's finally close enough to make a grab for its startled victim.

Chapter Two

TERRIBLE TEETH

QUIZ

The animal world is full of marvelous molars and fearsome fangs, but are the facts about some of nature's nastiest chompers true or false? Mark the your answers on another sheet of paper.

THE "FACTS"	TRUE	FALSE
1. A snail has more than 25,000 teeth.		
2. A walrus can walk on its teeth.		
3. Sharks don't use their teeth for chewing.		
4. The male angler fish uses his teeth to find the love of his life and never lets her go.		
5. Alligators will often give you a toothy grin.		
6. The blue whale has the largest teeth in the animal world.		
7. A spider chews its food before it swallows it.		

1. A SNAIL HAS MORE THAN 25,000 TEETH.

TRUE

A snail's ribbonlike tongue is lined with microscopic munchers that look like the spikes on the edge of a saw blade. The snail uses its tiny teeth to slice off morsels of food before digesting them.

2. A WALRUS CAN WALK ON ITS TEETH.

TRUE

Walruses use their two huge tusks, which are nearly 3 feet (1 m) long, to pull themselves out of the water. They can also use their teeth to help them "walk" across the ground. The walrus's scientific name (Odobenus rosmarus) means "tooth-walking sea horse," which is quite a mouthful!

3. SHARKS DON'T USE THEIR TEETH FOR CHEWING.

TRUE

While sharks can have up to 3,000 chompers in their mouths at a time, they really only use them to snatch and tear their food apart before gulping down the chunks.

4. THE MALE ANGLER FISH USES HIS TEETH TO FIND THE LOVE OF HIS LIFE AND NEVER LETS HER GO.

TRUE

When a male angler fish finds a female, he hangs on to her with his small, hooklike teeth and doesn't let her go. He releases a substance that digests the skin of her body and the skin of his mouth so they stick together. Over time the male gradually wastes away, losing his brain, internal organs, and even his eyes. And you thought getting your braces stuck mid-smooch was bad!

5. ALLIGATORS WILL OFTEN GIVE YOU A TOOTHY GRIN.

TRUE

Though an alligator's teeth are hidden when its mouth is closed, it often sits around with its mouth open in a "grin." You don't want to be around when an alligator is showing off its pearly whites. The force of its bite is about the same as getting crushed by a falling car!

6. THE BLUE WHALE HAS THE LARGEST TEETH IN THE ANIMAL WORLD.

FALSE

The blue whale is the largest animal on Earth, but it doesn't have any teeth. Instead, its mouth is filled with plates, called baleen, which are covered in bristles. The whale traps its food—tiny, shrimp like animals called krill—in the bristles and then gulps them down.

7. A SPIDER CHEWS ITS FOOD BEFORE IT SWALLOWS IT.

FALSE

A spider doesn't chew its food. When a spider finds an insect caught in its sticky web, it wraps the insect up in silk and uses its fangs to inject poison. When it is time to eat, the spider smears its victim with strong digestive juices and waits patiently for the snack to dissolve. When the insect has turned to mush, the spider sucks it up like bug soup. Yummy!

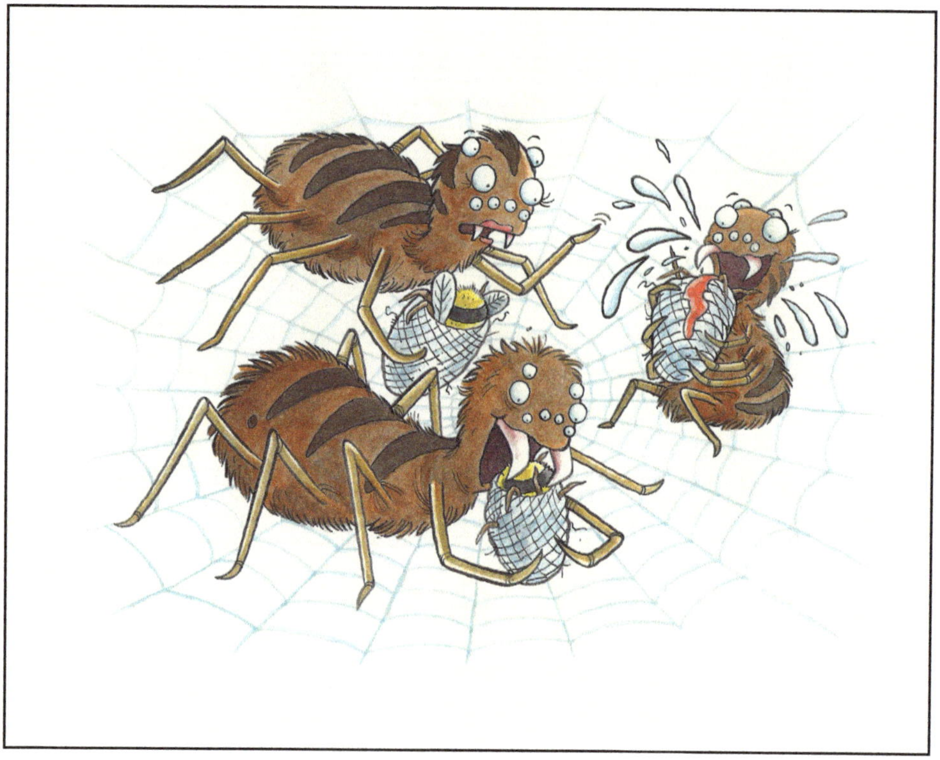

Chapter Three

EAT OR BE EATEN

QUIZ

Some creatures have terrible taste when it comes to food. Are these vomit-worthy facts hard or easy to swallow? Keep your answers on another sheet of paper.

THE "FACTS"	TRUE	FALSE
1. The Venus flytrap plant spits out things it doesn't like.	☐	☐
2. Koala babies eat their mother's poop.	☐	☐
3. The housefly throws up its food, then eats it again.	☐	☐
4. The red snapper fish has a sea louse for a tongue.	☐	☐
5. Rabbits eat their own poop.	☐	☐
6. Cows don't fart after eating.	☐	☐
7. The starfish's stomach is outside its body.	☐	☐

1. THE VENUS FLYTRAP PLANT SPITS OUT THINGS IT DOESN'T LIKE.

FALSE

The Venus flytrap has special pairs of leaves that are covered in tiny hairs and have spiny teeth along their edges. When a fly or insect touches the hairs, the two halves close, trapping the prey. However, there's a small gap around the edges, so if the prey is too tiny to bother with, it's allowed to escape.

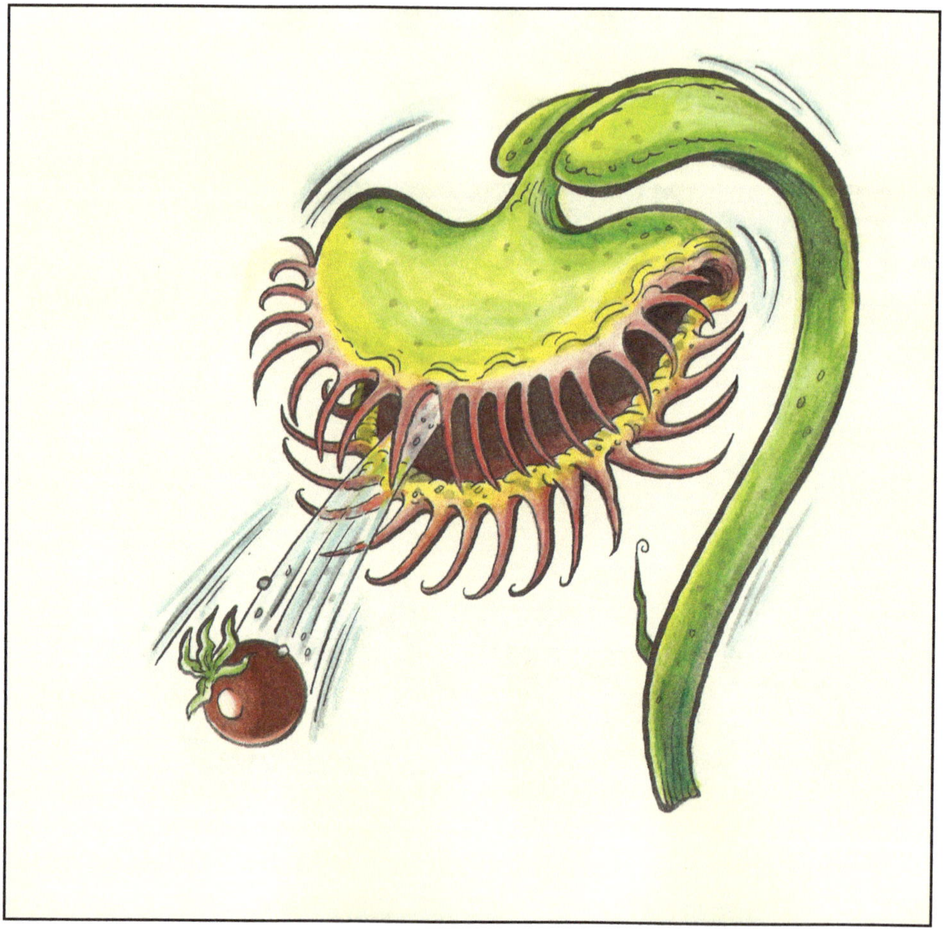

2. KOALA BABIES EAT THEIR MOTHER'S POOP.

TRUE

When a baby koala is ready to move on from its mother's milk, it needs to get used to a diet of eucalyptus leaves. These leaves contain poisons that would make a young koala very sick, so the mother koala produces a special poop with some of the poisons taken out, and the baby eats it.

3. THE HOUSEFLY THROWS UP ITS FOOD, THEN EATS IT AGAIN.

TRUE

A housefly can only eat liquid food. It spits digestive juices on the food to help dissolve it and then sucks it up. If the food hasn't dissolved fully, the fly regurgitates, or throws it up, and eats it again.

4. THE RED SNAPPER FISH HAS A SEA LOUSE FOR A TONGUE.

TRUE

A parasite is a creature that lives in or on another animal. Red snapper fish often have a parasite living in their mouths. This cringe-worthy creature sucks blood from the fish's tongue until the tongue withers and dies. Then the parasite takes the place of the tongue so that the fish can continue to eat. Every time the fish eats, the parasite keeps a little bit of the food for itself. Sneaky!

5. RABBITS EAT THEIR OWN POOP.

TRUE

Rabbits actually need to eat some of the stuff they poop out, called cecotropes. These poopy pellets have loads of good vitamins and help rabbits digest food. Tasty!

6. COWS DON'T FART AFTER EATING.

FALSE

A cow can eat up to 90 pounds (41 kg) of food a day, which gives it tons of gas. Cows are constantly burping and farting, releasing more than 79 gallons (300 L) of smelly methane gas every day. And with more than a billion cows on the planet, that's a lot of gas!

7. THE STARFISH'S STOMACH IS OUTSIDE ITS BODY.

FALSE

The starfish doesn't have a stomach on the outside of its body, but it can turn itself inside out when it wants to eat something that's too big to fit in its mouth. So the starfish pushes its stomach out through its mouth to digest the food. When it's done, the starfish puts its tummy away again.

Chapter Four

SERIOUS SURVIVAL SKILLS

QUIZ

The natural world is filled with tough reptiles, indestructible insects, and other amazingly adaptable organisms. But are these facts about the strongest survivors true or false? Mark your answers on a separate sheet of paper, then turn the page to discover the truth!

THE "FACTS"

	TRUE	FALSE
1. An opossum is a furry faker that plays dead to escape predators.	☐	☐
2. The Spanish ribbed newt is known as Robin Hood because it protects itself with bows and arrows.	☐	☐
3. Crocodiles are such great survivors, they even lived when dinosaurs roamed the Earth.	☐	☐
4. Lizards shed their tails to escape predators.	☐	☐
5. No plant is tough enough to survive in Antarctica.	☐	☐
6. Cockroaches can survive without their heads.	☐	☐
7. Sharks are so adaptable, they have even swum in space.	☐	☐

1. AN OPOSSUM IS A FURRY FAKER THAT PLAYS DEAD TO ESCAPE PREDATORS.

TRUE

These furry fighters are fine actors. When they feel threatened, they pretend to be dead with Hollywood-worthy acting skills, known as "playing possum." An opossum lies on the ground with its tongue hanging out of its mouth and releases a stinky smell to keep animals from checking it out. Most animals don't like to scavenge, which means they don't like to eat meat that is already dead when they find it. So playing dead keeps opossums safe from predators.

2. THE SPANISH RIBBED NEWT IS KNOWN AS ROBIN HOOD BECAUSE IT PROTECTS ITSELF WITH BOWS AND ARROWS.

FALSE

The Spanish ribbed newt doesn't use a set of bows and arrows, but this tough little fighter goes to extreme lengths to protect itself. When an enemy comes near, the ribbed newt pushes its ribs through its skin to make a row of sharp, pointed arrows. Each "arrow" is tipped with poison from the newt's skin to keep predators away.

3. CROCODILES ARE SUCH GREAT SURVIVORS, THEY EVEN LIVED WHEN DINOSAURS ROAMED THE EARTH.

TRUE

Crocodiles have been on the planet for over 200 million years. They existed alongside dinosaurs—but while dinosaurs became extinct 65 million years ago, crocodiles survived. These cunning creatures have keen senses, are amazing hunters, and can go without food for long periods of time, making them one of Earth's super-survivors.

4. LIZARDS SHED THEIR TAILS TO ESCAPE PREDATORS.

TRUE

If a predator grabs a lizard by its tail, very often the tail is all it will get to eat. The lizard is able to shed its tail, leaving it wriggling about in the surprised predator's mouth. The lizard itself escapes to live another day . . . and, eventually, grow a new tail.

5. NO PLANT IS TOUGH ENOUGH TO SURVIVE IN ANTARCTICA.

FALSE

Antarctica is a frozen desert, and only the most stubborn creatures can survive there. However, quite a few kinds of simple plants, such as mosses and tiny plant-like organisms called algae, do live in some parts of the Antarctic. Lichens, which are half algae and half fungus, are even tougher. They have been found close to the South Pole, coping with the longest, darkest, coldest winter in the world.

6. COCKROACHES CAN SURVIVE WITHOUT THEIR HEADS.

TRUE

Since they can survive for many days without food and water, cockroaches don't need their heads to keep going. Unlike humans, cockroaches don't have a nose on their head. Instead, they breathe through parts of their body. A cockroach's body seals over a cut quickly, so a cockroach won't bleed to death when it loses its head. It can survive for several weeks without one. Even grosser, the head can live on for hours even without the body. Talk about a brawny bug!

7. SHARKS ARE SO ADAPTABLE, THEY HAVE EVEN SWUM IN SPACE.

FALSE

Sharks haven't made it to space, but an amazingly adaptable fish called the mummichog became the first fish in space. It swam in zero gravity on a mission in 1973. It is probably the world's toughest fish, since it is also able to live in fresh- or saltwater—something most of its finned friends can't do—and can survive in badly polluted waters. That's one strong swimmer.

Chapter Five

SUPERPOWERS

QUIZ

Some of the world's cleverest creatures have amazing abilities, but can you tell the real superpowers from the fakes? Write down your answers on another piece of paper.

THE "FACTS"	TRUE	FALSE
1. A bloodhound's sense of smell is thousands of times stronger than a human's.	☐	☐
2. The short-horned lizard spits blood to frighten its enemies.	☐	☐
3. The torpedo fish electrocutes its prey.	☐	☐
4. A snakebite can kill an elephant but not a honey badger.	☐	☐
5. Geckos have super climbing powers that allow them to scale slippery surfaces, such as glass.	☐	☐
6. Jellyfish can live forever.	☐	☐
7. The hairworm can control a cricket's mind.	☐	☐

1. A BLOODHOUND'S SENSE OF SMELL IS THOUSANDS OF TIMES STRONGER THAN A HUMAN'S.

TRUE

These superdogs have such a keen sense of smell that they are often seen as heroes. They have 4 billion smell-detecting cells in their noses, and the

wrinkles around their faces help guide any stray smell particles into their big nostrils. Bloodhounds are used by the police, because their sensitive snouts can help track down missing people and sniff out criminals.

2. THE SHORT-HORNED LIZARD SPITS BLOOD TO FRIGHTEN ITS ENEMIES.

FALSE

It's actually weirder than that. A short-horned lizard squirts blood from its eyes when it is attacked and can shoot the disgusting-tasting liquid up to 10 feet (3 m). It can also inflate its body so that it looks like a spiny balloon.

3. THE TORPEDO FISH ELECTROCUTES ITS PREY.

TRUE

The torpedo fish, also known as the electric ray, can produce up to 200 volts of electricity, which is enough power to kill its prey immediately. Supplying the shock is a pair of organs located in each of the fins behind this fierce fish's eyes.

4. A SNAKEBITE CAN KILL AN ELEPHANT BUT NOT A HONEY BADGER.

TRUE

The honey badger is one of the fiercest animals in the world. This fearless hunter will steal prey from venomous snakes and even tackle the snakes themselves. A bite from a puff adder—Africa's most dangerous snake—contains enough venom to kill five humans, but for a honey badger it just stings a little for a few hours.

5. GECKOS HAVE SUPER CLIMBING POWERS THAT ALLOW THEM TO SCALE SLIPPERY SURFACES, SUCH AS GLASS.

TRUE

These clever climbers have millions of microscopic hairs on the bottom of their feet. The hairs act like a super-sticky glue and allow geckos to cling to almost any kind of surface. The hairs aren't actually covered in any kind of sticky substance, so the geckos don't get stuck, and they don't leave a messy trail as they climb, either.

6. JELLYFISH CAN LIVE FOREVER.

TRUE

A certain kind of jellyfish can live forever. . . . Well, sort of. Scientists say that these tiny jellyfish can age backward. That is, once they are fully grown, some of the jellyfish transform back into a polyp, which is the form of a baby jellyfish. They can then grow into adults again. This jellyfish is the only animal capable of this, and it can repeat this cycle over and over. So it's almost as though they can live forever!

7. THE HAIRWORM CAN CONTROL A CRICKET'S MIND.

TRUE

This powerful parasite makes its home inside a cricket, where it produces a cocktail of chemicals that affects the way the cricket thinks and behaves. Eventually, the hairworm convinces the cricket to plunge into water. Sadly, the cricket drowns. The hairworm, however, emerges from the dead cricket and looks for a mate in the water.

Chapter Six

PECULIAR PARENTING

QUIZ

There are lots of miserable mothers, dastardly dads, and some perfect parents in the natural world, but can you tell which are the facts and which are lies? Decide whether the facts are true or false, and write your answers on a separate sheet of paper.

THE "FACTS"	TRUE	FALSE
1. The female emperor penguin lays her egg on the ice and leaves it all alone there until it hatches.	☐	☐
2. The Siamese fighting fish protects its young by blowing bubbles.	☐	☐
3. A bird called the hooded grebe lays one egg at a time so she can love and spoil just one chick.	☐	☐
4. Black eagle mothers let their kids fight bloody battles.	☐	☐
5. Female grizzly bears kill their cubs.	☐	☐
6. Elephant seals would rather adopt than look after their own babies.	☐	☐
7. The Nile crocodile eats its young while they are still in their eggs.	☐	☐
8. Male sea horses can bear as many as 600 baby sea horses.	☐	☐

1. THE FEMALE EMPEROR PENGUIN LAYS HER EGG ON THE ICE AND LEAVES IT ALL ALONE THERE UNTIL IT HATCHES.

FALSE

After the mother penguin lays an egg, she goes off to find food. But the father puts the egg on top of his feet and pulls a flap of skin over it to keep it warm. Then the dad stands in the harsh winter and waits for it to hatch. If the egg falls on to the freezing ice, the baby penguin will die.

2. THE SIAMESE FIGHTING FISH PROTECTS ITS YOUNG BY BLOWING BUBBLES.

TRUE

The male Siamese fighting fish is an amazing dad. He makes a nest of bubbles to protect the eggs laid by his mate. He watches over the eggs and constantly repairs the nest by spitting more bubbles. If an egg falls out of the bubble nest, he carefully puts it back. However, the baby fish need to swim away soon after hatching, because the kind dad may try to eat them!

3. A BIRD CALLED THE HOODED GREBE LAYS ONE EGG AT A TIME SO SHE CAN LOVE AND SPOIL JUST ONE CHICK.

FALSE

Birds called hooded grebes lay two eggs at a time, and both parents keep them warm until hatching time. The egg that hatches first becomes mama's cherished chick. In fact, both parents abandon the other egg as soon as the first egg hatches, leaving baby number two to fend for itself.

4. BLACK EAGLE MOTHERS LET THEIR KIDS FIGHT BLOODY BATTLES.

TRUE

When baby black eagles fight, the naughty kids don't get a time-out. Their mom lets them fight violently—to the death. Two eggs are laid, but the parents can only catch enough prey to bring up one chick. They let the two fight it out so that the stronger baby—almost always the older one—survives.

5. FEMALE GRIZZLY BEARS KILL THEIR CUBS.

FALSE

The female grizzly bear is one of the most protective mothers on the planet. She will go to great lengths to keep her cubs safe. Male grizzly bears often kill the cubs of other males, so to keep them safe, moms take their cubs to remote areas where there aren't many other bears around.

6. ELEPHANT SEALS WOULD RATHER ADOPT THAN LOOK AFTER THEIR OWN BABIES.

FALSE

The northern elephant seal is a great mother. She takes care of her own baby, or pup, often going without food just to stay close. But if she loses her pup, she will go to any length to get another. She'll adopt orphan pups or even steal one from another mother!

7. THE NILE CROCODILE EATS ITS YOUNG WHILE THEY ARE STILL IN THEIR EGGS.

FALSE

A mother crocodile watches over her eggs, waiting for the moment when the tiny crocs make chirruping sounds inside. Then she takes an egg gently in her mouth and rolls it around to help it hatch. After the eggs have hatched, she continues to look after her babies until they are old enough to feed themselves.

8. MALE SEA HORSES CAN BEAR AS MANY AS 600 BABY SEA HORSES.

TRUE

In the world of sea horses, the role of baby bearing is carried out by the male, who can have anywhere from 200 to 600 babies at one time! To impress a potential mate and show off his birthing pouch, a male sea horse will fill up his pouch with as much water as he can to indicate his strength and ability to carry a load of baby sea horses through three weeks of pregnancy and 72 hours of labor. After the babies are born, the female assumes the role of finding food for them. Within just a few weeks the male sea horse will fill up its pouch once more to let the female know he is ready to do it all over again.

Chapter Seven

HORRIBLE HABITS

QUIZ

If you think your friend's nose-picking habit is disgusting, wait until you see what some of these animals are up to. Decide which are the true facts. Then turn to pages 35–38 to find out the truth.

THE "FACTS"	TRUE	FALSE
1. Camels spit at people or animals that threaten them.	☐	☐
2. Bush babies drink their own pee.	☐	☐
3. Hagfish cover themselves in mucus.	☐	☐
4. Vampire bats drink blood only from dead animals.	☐	☐
5. The boa constrictor swallows large pigs—whole!	☐	☐
6. Cats swallow their own hair and cough up furry balls of it.	☐	☐
7. Dogs sniff each other's behinds.	☐	☐

1. CAMELS SPIT AT PEOPLE OR ANIMALS THAT THREATEN THEM.

FALSE

When a camel feels threatened, it brings up the contents of its stomach, along with saliva, and spits it at whatever or whoever is bothering it. The vile vomit is meant to distract, pester, or surprise whatever is threatening the camel. While camels will aim a stomach-churning mouthful at people when they are very annoyed, this spiteful spitting is mostly used to settle disputes with other camels over things like whose turn it is to drink at the watering hole.

2. BUSH BABIES DRINK THEIR OWN PEE.

FALSE

Bush babies are small, fluffy animals related to monkeys. They look far too cute to have a horrible habit, but one very unpleasant thing they do is catch their pee in their hands. When a bush baby climbs and jumps through the trees, every time it grabs a branch, it leaves a smelly handprint of pee behind, which tells other bush babies where it has been. Pee is very important in bush babies' love lives, too—a male bush baby lets a female know that he likes her by peeing on her. Charming!

3. HAGFISH COVER THEMSELVES IN MUCUS.

TRUE

The hagfish has been named the most disgusting sea creature in the world, because it covers itself with huge amounts of sticky mucus to escape predators. It also rubs slime on its prey to stop it from breathing. Mmm! Booger-covered snack, anyone? When the hagfish has more mucus over its body than even it can bear and wants to get rid of some of the goo, it ties its long, thin body in a knot, then passes the knot down its length to scrape off the gloopy gunk.

4. VAMPIRE BATS DRINK BLOOD ONLY FROM DEAD ANIMALS.

FALSE

Vampire bats prefer warm blood from living animals or humans. They wait until their victim is asleep, and then they search for a part of the body that isn't covered with hair so they can get a good bite. When they have made a hole in the skin with their fangs, the bats scarf down the blood like a warm glass of milk. Their saliva contains a chemical

called draculin, which stops the blood from clotting as it would normally, so the wound continues to bleed for a long time. If some vampire bats in the colony don't manage to feed in the night, the others will help them out with a meal of vomited-up blood.

5. THE BOA CONSTRICTOR SWALLOWS LARGE PIGS—WHOLE!

TRUE

This scary snake has terrible table manners and never chews its food before swallowing—not even if it's a pig or a deer. The boa constrictor overpowers its prey by squeezing the life out of it. Then it opens its mouth to an enormous size and crams the animal in whole. This leaves the boa with a huge bulge in its belly, so it slithers slowly and carefully away to a quiet spot, where it spends a week or longer lying around, gradually digesting its monster meal.

6. CATS SWALLOW THEIR OWN HAIR AND COUGH UP FURRY BALLS OF IT.

TRUE

Cats are quite enthusiastic about cleaning themselves. When a cat wants to get clean, it licks its fur, but loads of tiny hairs get stuck in the cat's rough tongue, especially if it is a long-haired cat. Those hairs get swallowed and can upset the kitty's tummy. When too much hair is swallowed, the cat pukes up a disgusting lumpy mass of stuck-together hair. If you don't want your cat to suffer from fur balls, give it a good combing from time to time to help get rid of all the loose fur.

7. DOGS SNIFF EACH OTHER'S BEHINDS.

TRUE

Dogs have an extra gland around their bottoms that gives off a smell. Each dog releases a unique scent, so smelling one another's bottoms is a way of recognizing and meeting other dogs. Scientists say that dogs can learn a lot from sniffing other dogs' bottoms. Occasionally, the glands can get blocked up, which is painful for the dog, and the stinky gunk inside needs to be emptied out by a vet. The vet will probably want to wear nose plugs when carrying out this revolting task.

Chapter Eight

BONKERS BIOLOGY

QUIZ

Sometimes the truth about biology is stranger than fiction. But can you tell which facts are real and which are fiendish fakes? Make your choices, and keep track of them on another piece of paper.

THE "FACTS"	TRUE	FALSE
1. The liger and the pizzly bear are examples of crossbred animals.	☐	☐
2. In the 17th century, boys at a school in Eton, England, were punished if they didn't smoke.	☐	☐
3. The skeletons of babies and adult humans have the same number of parts.	☐	☐
4 Fruits and vegetables that are super rich in vitamins have been developed by scientists	☐	☐
5. All forms of bacteria are harmful to humans..	☐	☐
6. No two humans have the same DNA.	☐	☐
7. Mold is nature's way of recycling.	☐	☐
8. Coral from the sea can replace bones in the human body.	☐	☐

1. THE LIGER AND THE PIZZLY BEAR ARE EXAMPLES OF CROSSBRED ANIMALS.

TRUE

Strange as it may seem, some wild animals can be crossbred in captivity. So a lion and tiger may have a baby called a "liger." A "pizzly bear" is a polar bear bred with a grizzly bear. Other hybrids include the zonkey (zebra/donkey), the cama (camal/llama), and the wholphin (whale/dolphin).

2. IN THE 17TH CENTURY, BOYS AT A SCHOOL IN ETON, ENGLAND, WERE PUNISHED IF THEY DIDN'T SMOKE.

TRUE

Nowadays smoking is known to be harmful to health, and any school kid caught puffing on a cigarette is likely to be dragged over the coals by their teacher. But in the 17th century, when plague was rife, people noticed that the owners of tobacco shops didn't seem to get sick. So at Eton, a school near London, boys were punished if they didn't smoke pipe tobacco.

3. THE SKELETONS OF BABY AND ADULT HUMANS HAVE THE SAME NUMBER OF PARTS.

FALSE

When babies are born, their skeletons contain nearly 300 parts. As they grow older, some of the parts fuse together, and by adulthood the skeleton consists of 206 bones.

4. FRUITS AND VEGETABLES THAT ARE SUPER RICH IN VITAMINS HAVE BEEN DEVELOPED BY SCIENTISTS.

TRUE

Scientists have started to develop genetically modified crops (GM crops) that are resistant to disease and give higher yields. They are also working on genetically modified fruits and vegetables, mostly to help them stay fresher longer and to improve the taste. It's in its early days, but so far, purple tomatoes have been created that are rich in chemicals said to prevent cancer. Scientists are also working to produce "edible vaccines" in bananas, but it will be a while before they appear on our tables. There is a lot of debate around the science of GM food. Many people aren't eager to eat it, and they worry about the unknown negative effects of eating GM food over many years.

5. ALL FORMS OF BACTERIA ARE HARMFUL TO HUMANS.

FALSE

Bacteria are microscopic single-celled organisms. They are found everywhere, even inside our bodies. Some bacteria are helpful to humans. For example, within our colons there are more than 500 different species of bacteria that help to keep us healthy and digest food. They also fight the harmful bacteria that can make us sick.

6. NO TWO HUMANS HAVE THE SAME DNA.

FALSE

A chemical called DNA is contained in each cell of your body. It acts as a chemical code of instructions telling your body how to grow. It is inherited from your parents. Each person's DNA is unique, except for the DNA of identical twins. These twins grow from the same egg, which splits to form the two embryos that will grow into two babies. Each embryo contains the same DNA, which is why identical twins often look alike. There are some differences, though; identical twins have similar, but not identical, fingerprints.

7. MOLD IS NATURE'S WAY OF RECYCLING.

TRUE

Mold is a type of fungus. It grows from tiny particles, or "spores," floating in the air. Mold is useful in nature because it helps to get rid of organic matter, such as fruits, vegetables, and leaves, by rotting it and returning it to the soil. The downside of mold is that because it destroys the things it grows on, when it grows in homes, it can be a real problem. It can mess up walls and furniture. Sometimes it can make people sick, since the spores can cause allergies, asthma attacks, and even chest infections.

8. CORAL FROM THE SEA CAN REPLACE BONES IN THE HUMAN BODY.

TRUE

The chemistry of coral is so close to human bones that it is being used to repair or replace them. To repair a fracture, doctors inject treated coral that's been formed into a paste. After a couple of hours, the paste dries and is as hard as the human bone and melds almost seamlessly with the human skeleton. In fact, this alternative treatment has become so effective that it may completely replace traditional metal plates, pins, and screws someday.

YOUR SCORE

Keep a record of how many answers you got right in each section in the chart below. There are 58 in all. Then add up your scores to determine your grand total.

Bizarre Beasties	
Terrible Teeth	
Eat or Be Eaten	
Serious Survival Skills	
Superpowers	
Peculiar Parenting	
Horrible Habits	
Bonkers Biology	
TOTAL	

GLOSSARY

baleen—A filter-type feeding system used by many whale species. This filter feeds the whale while removing anything not edible.

colony—A group of people or animals that live together.

DNA (deoxyribonucleic acid)—A molecule in living organisms that carries information about reproduction, genetics, development and function.

gland—An organ in a human or animal's body that secretes particular chemical substances for use in the body or its surroundings.

lichen—A simple, slow-growing plant that typically grows on walls, rocks, or trees (also known as moss).

parasite—An organism that lives inside another organism and that gets its nutrients from the host.

proboscis—An elongated appendage that grows from the head of an animal, typically tubular and used for sucking or vacuuming up food, or water.

spore—A single-celled way of asexual reproduction often used by plants and algae.

uropod—The final appendage on many crustaceans.

venom—A poison secreted by an organism that is designed to help it subdue prey.

FURTHER READING

BOOKS

1000 Strange But True Animal Facts (Discovery Kids). New York, NY: Parragon Books, 2014.

Dawn Cusick. *Get the Scoop on Animal Poop: From Lions to Tapeworms: 251 Cool Facts about Scat, Frass, Dung, and More!* Bournemouth, United Kingdom: Imagine Publishing, 2013.

Loy, Jessica. *Weird and Wild Animal Facts.* New York, NY: Henry Holt and Co., 2015.

WEBSITES

www.sciencekids.co.nz/sciencefacts/animals.html
Learn fun animal facts.

kids.nationalgeographic.com/animals/
Read articles, watch videos, and view photos of animals.

nationalzoo.si.edu/
Explore the official website of the National Zoo in Washington, DC.

INDEX